IMAGES OF LONDON

GREENWICH
CENTRE OF THE WORLD

IMAGES OF LONDON

GREENWICH
CENTRE OF THE WORLD

DAVID RAMZAN

For friends and family long gone, for those who still remain, and for those who are still to come. Time immemorial.

First published in 2007 by Tempus Publishing

Reprinted in 2009 by
The History Press
The Mill, Brimscombe Port,
Stroud, Gloucestershire, GL5 2QG
www.thehistorypress.co.uk

British Library Cataloguing in Publication Data.
A catalogue record for this book is available from the British Library.

ISBN 978 0 7524 4260 0

Typesetting and origination by
Tempus Publishing Limited.
Printed and bound in Great Britain by Athenaeum Press Ltd., Gateshead, Tyne & Wear.

Contents

Acknowledgements

The majority of images used in this publication are from the archives of the local history library in the Greenwich Heritage Centre based at Woolwich Arsenal. I should like to thank all the staff at the library without whose help I could not have possibly compiled this book. Some images are from my own family collection and if for any reason I have not accredited any photographs to people or organisations as necessary or failed to trace any copyright holders, then I should like to apologise for this oversight. I should like to thank all those who have advised me on specific historical points about Greenwich including the Greenwich Heritage Centre, the Greenwich Industrial Heritage Society, the National Maritime Museum, Greenwich Police Station, Greenwich Magistrates Court, the Metropolitan Police Historical Museum, Doris Ramzan, Helen Ashby, Doreen Ramzan and Bob Headley.

Photographic credits: The Greenwich Heritage Centre, the Collections of the Ramzan and Peachey families, Valerie Harvey, P.O. Driscoll and the Thames Sailing Barge Trust.

Greenwich Time, the twenty-four hour clock on the Royal Observatory boundary wall. All the time zones around the world are measured from this spot.

Introduction

Greenwich, Centre of the World

Greenwich: Latitude 51:28 North – Longitude 0:00 East, Greenwich (Greenport or harbour) landing place of the Danes 1011; murder spot of Alphege, archbishop of Canterbury 1012; Royal Manor of Henry V 1414; site of a Royal Palace built 1427; birthplace of Henry VIII 1491 and of his daughters, Mary 1516, and Elizabeth 1533; Royal Observatory established and building completed by Sir Christopher Wren 1675; the Royal Naval Hospital founded by Queen Mary 1694; the body of General James Wolfe, hero of the battle of Quebec, returned to lie in state 1759; first Ordnance Survey map produced showing the Meridian Line 1801; Admiral Lord Nelson's body laid in state Royal Naval Hospital 1806; the largest underwater tunnel in the world opened at Blackwall 1897; the Millennium celebration festivities were held here in the year 2000. Greenwich, where East meets West, and people from all parts of the globe come to stand astride the famous Meridian Line.

I was born in Greenwich in 1954 at St Alphege's Hospital situated just to the east of the Meridian Line. My parents came from the area as did most of my family, if not directly from Greenwich, at least within a five-mile radius of the Meridian Line.

One exception was my father's father, who journeyed from India by way of the Royal Navy, eventually settling in Greenwich in the early part of the 1900s. My grandfather joined the Navy as a boy sailor to break free from a land of rebellion and to seek his fortune in what was to him, and many others who journeyed to Britain, a land of opportunity. For a while he served on HMS *Victory*, a training ship at that time, before finding his way to Greenwich and marrying a local girl whose family had been residents in the area for many years.

Greenwich at the turn of the twentieth century was a place where you could make a good living. There was work to be had in many of the commercial or industrial businesses in the town or on the river. The military had been based in and around Greenwich for hundreds of years, and offered the opportunity of work to local people especially in the armaments factories in Woolwich.

Greenwich was a truly cosmopolitan part of London. Ships from far-off shores would tie up at riverside wharves, bringing in goods from all corners of the world with their foreign crews frequenting the pubs once found on almost every riverside street corner.

Markets and shops sold everything a Greenwich resident could want, from fruit to furniture. With the latest transport systems operating out of Greenwich, from trains, trams and paddle steamers, people could travel more freely to more destinations than ever before.

Tourists visiting Greenwich could take trip on a steamer along the river, spend a day in the park to watch the royal deer, or visit the legendary Elizabethan Oak. Perhaps in the evening they would take a trip to the theatre followed by a fish supper at one of the famous taverns by the river Thames.

Greenwich was not only a place for people to visit, it was becoming one of London's more fashionable places to live. While the lower part of Greenwich housed a majority of working-class people living in rows of Victorian houses, the higher class of person could be found living in West Greenwich and Blackheath in the more luxurious Regency style properties.

My initial interest regarding the history and heritage of Greenwich came about by way of a piece of my own family history involving one of those houses on Blackheath. A great uncle on my father's side of the family was a police officer in Greenwich during the late 1800s. One night while out on duty he foiled an attempted break-in of a smart residential house on Blackheath. Although shot and wounded by a bullet fired from the burglar's revolver, he grappled with the assailant and held him down until two other officers arrived. The burglar turned out to be the notorious Victorian villain Charlie Peace, who was in fact my great-grandmother's godfather, on my mother's side of the family.

The Regency and Edwardian houses on Blackheath are still there although most have been turned into apartments and flats. However, as the years have gone by the Victorian and Edwardian houses that once occupied the lower part of Greenwich have gradually been replaced by newly built flats and apartments. Some are designed to reflect the heritage of Greenwich; others seem to have been built without much thought at all. In the 1950s, many new buildings were erected, replacing those destroyed in the air raids of the Second World War. As the old industries were closing down, modern factories units made of pre-fabricated materials were replacing them.

It seems planning consent was virtually non-existent during the time Greenwich was being 'modernised' – the buildings that survived the bombing raids were being pulled down and replaced by functional, cost-effective properties. Today most of the houses, shops, and warehouses that were destroyed by the new development plans of the 1950s and 1960s would be protected, renovated and preserved for posterity. Alas, it is too late for some of these buildings, the images of which appear in this publication, and can now only be seen in old black and white photographs.

There are pockets of Greenwich that still retain the charm of bygone days and a lucrative market has grown up within the film industry with regard to the hire of period locations. Many film production agencies come to Greenwich to use the town's buildings, streets and historical sites as backdrops and they pay very well to do so.

One production from years ago, *The List of Adrian Messenger* starring Robert Mitcham, Kirk Douglas, Tony Curtis, Frank Sinatra, and Burt Lancaster, to name just a few top 1950s stars, was shot on location in the streets of east Greenwich down by the Thames and close to the house where I grew up. The buildings in the film showed a part of Greenwich that had not changed for at least 100 years, with rows of terraced houses, corner shops and riverside pubs. It was an area where I spent many hours as a child playing with my friends, some who actually appeared in the film as extras.

Whilst carrying out research for this publication, and looking through hundreds of period photographs and prints of Greenwich, I have come to realise how much of the area's heritage has been lost, and even the modern streets of today seem somehow more shabby than in those early photographs. People in Greenwich at the turn of the twentieth century seem to have had a pride in the places they worked and lived – there is no graffiti on the walls and rubbish-strewn streets seem to have been at a minimum. People worked in, and for their community, and even though crime was part of a way of life, the police were at least out on the streets showing the face of law and enforcement. The late Victorian, early Georgian Greenwich seemed a much simpler place and time to have lived, with people working and residing in their local surroundings and families living in close proximity.

Today's modern society has changed completely – in many cases our work and home life are located miles apart; families move away and move on. In the next few years Greenwich will see a complete change with regard to regeneration in housing, working opportunities and new businesses. People will move into the area as new residents. Many of them, in all probability, not knowing the Greenwich of long ago, and I hope this publication will show them what a wonderful place Greenwich was, and still is today.

The Royal Borough of Greenwich, designated world heritage site – centre of the world.

David Ramzan
February 2007

one

A Brief History in Time

Observatory, Greenwich.

If you stand in Greenwich Park and look down from the top of One Tree Hill you will see in front of you a panoramic view of living history – the great 'U' bend in the river Thames where Vikings once moored their longships, the Royal Naval College originally built as a palace for a Queen, the Millennium Dome, the site where great ships were built and the

Placentia, Greenwich's first royal palace depicted in an engraving from the mid-1700s. Humphrey, Duke of Gloucester and Regent of England started to build a palace near to the site of the present Royal Naval College after the manor of Greenwich was passed to him in 1427. The original name was to

clipper ship *Cutty Sark* landlocked in what was once the medieval quarter of Greenwich. The park and surrounding area has a history going back to ancient times and wherever your gaze takes you, there you will find a part of Greenwich that has its own fascinating story to tell.

be Bella Court, but on his death in 1447 the manor reverted to the crown. The palace was renamed Placentia and became the principal palace of Henry VI. The birthplace of Henry VIII in 1491 and Elizabeth I in 1533, it fell into disrepair and was demolished in the mid-1600s.

The history of Greenwich goes back much further than the times of the first Tudor royals who lived in Greenwich. Ancient British burial grounds have been found in Greenwich Park, some believed to be those of British chieftains and many Roman remains have also been excavated in the park grounds. This photograph from 1920 shows Herbert Jones and his wife overseeing a dig in Greenwich Park where many roman artefacts were discovered and are now stored at the British Museum.

Ancient remains have been located all over Blackheath, with some interesting caverns discovered by workmen in 1780. They were thought to have been dene holes used by locals as hiding places from the Danish invaders. At Maidstone Hill on Blackheath, a series of caves and tunnels run through Point Hill, shown in this drawing from the time the caverns were discovered, and were dug out from the chalk within the hill. It is rumoured that some of the tunnels stretch as far as Chislehurst caves in Kent, but so far this has never been proved.

During the mid-1800s drinking parties and masked balls were held in some of the larger caverns as depicted in an illustration of the time, but were soon closed down after the party revellers were getting too out of hand. Some of these hidden caves were also used during this time as storehouses for stolen goods. Limekilns were also discovered in the area with many tunnels running all across the heath. In 2003, part of the roadway on Blackheath Hill collapsed into some of the chalk pits, causing chaos with the road system for several months.

Many of the tunnels found within the boundaries of park and heath are actually man-made brick conduits. It was thought that most of these tunnels acted as watercourses for the Palace of Placentia built during the 1400s. The photograph taken during excavations in the mid-1900s shows part of a tunnel running out towards an opening in Greenwich Park. Some tunnels are up to a quarter of a mile in length with several access points found at ground level. As children, my friends and I would regularly try to find the hidden entrances to this secret labyrinth of tunnels. Although the tunnels are still navigational the local authorities have restricted their access.

Greenwich's own castle, *c.* 1790. Just outside of the walls of Greenwich Park on the junction of Westcombe Park Road and Maze Hill stands Sir John Vanbrugh's house. This famous architect and dramatist of the time designed the house in the guise of a medieval castle. The structure was completed in 1717, and Vanbrugh gave it the name of the Bastille House because at one time he'd been locked up in the original Bastille accused of being a British spy. The house, now called Vanbrugh Castle, was privately owned after his death, then used as a school for some time before reverting to private ownership once again.

The name Greenwich was thought to have come from the Danish derivative 'green reach' or 'harbour'. Since early times Greenwich had been an anchorage for numerous fleets from across the waters, whether invading or trading. It is no surprise that Greenwich became synonymous with seafarers for hundreds of years. This shows recruits from the Royal Hospital School (now the Maritime Museum) around 1905, with the training ship *Fame* in the background where thousands of young sailors would have learned their seamanship skills.

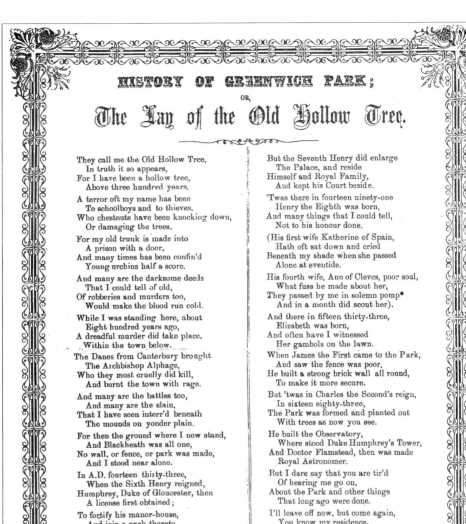

A very old resident of Greenwich Park had many tales to tell of the history and legend of a Greenwich of long ago. The stories, most based on fact, were printed in verse at the turn of the century as the thoughts and memories of Queen Elizabeth's Oak, once a landmark in the centre of Greenwich Park. The tree was in fact a chestnut, and died in the nineteenth century, but was held upright by the ivy that entwined the hollow remains. The old tree finally collapsed completely during 1991 and a new sapling was planted to replace it.

Latter-day cadets during the Second World War form a guard of honour for the First Sea Lord A.V. Alexander and Col. Knox, Head of the American Navy, as they make their way from Greenwich pier to the Royal Naval College during the 1940s. Up until the start of this century, Greenwich had been a training base for Navy personnel for almost 150 years. The Royal Naval College designed by Christopher Wren and built between 1696 and 1712, was originally a seamen's hospital before transferring to a naval establishment in 1873.

Another Francis is knighted by a Queen Elizabeth at the Royal Naval College. In 1967 residents of Greenwich watch Her Majesty Queen Elizabeth II knight Sir Francis Chichester using the same sword that the Queen Elizabeth I used to knight Sir Francis Drake. Thousands of people lined the streets to be part of this historic occasion when the round-the-world record-breaking yachtsman received his knighthood. His boat *Gipsy Moth IV* was moored in dry dock at Greenwich for several years before being restored and returned to the sea.

In 1806, the body of Admiral Lord Nelson laid in state at the Painted Hall in Greenwich Hospital before the river funeral procession took him to his final resting place up river to St Paul's Cathedral. Almost fifty years on, a relic of the battle of Trafalgar, Nelson's waistcoat and topcoat worn on the deck of the *Victory* was found by way of Lady Hamilton, in the private ownership of the widow of a

THE COAT WORN BY NELSON, AT THE BATTLE OF TRAFALGAR.

THE WAISTCOAT.

local alderman of London. On hearing they were for sale, HRH Price Albert, husband of Queen Victoria, bought them and donated them to the Greenwich Hospital for posterity. The images were produced in news publications during the mid-1800s publicising Prince Albert's act of generosity.

George IV leaving the Royal Military Academy in Woolwich after a visit in 1913. The military has had a presence within the area of Greenwich for hundreds of years. In 1741 the board of ordinance at Woolwich Arsenal, founded and supported the academy. It was established to train potential officers for the Royal Artillery and Royal Engineers.

A unit from the Royal Regiment of Artillery, formed in 1716, were stationed in barracks at Woolwich Arsenal. The Woolwich Arsenal site had been manufacturing armaments since Tudor times, and was the oldest and biggest establishment of its kind in the whole of Britain. During the Second World War almost 40,000 workers from the area were employed in the manufacture of arms. The armed forces were a large part of the community within the Boroughs of Greenwich and Woolwich.

The Rotunda, a circular building near the Woolwich barracks, once housed a display of guns from the Royal Artillery. This structure was originally a tent that was erected to celebrate the defeat of Napoleon at the festivities in London. In 1816 it was moved to Woolwich, then converted into a permanent building by the architect John Nash in 1920. The guns once on display there have now been moved to a museum on the site of the Woolwich Arsenal.

The 40th Foot Regiment on manoeuvres at Woolwich, 1894. This light infantry regiment fought under Gen. James Wolf at the battle of Quebec in 1759. Wolfe, one time resident of Blackheath, was killed in the battle and his body was returned to be buried in the family vault at St Alphege's church, Greenwich.

Ships and shipping had been an integral part of the lives of Greenwich residents, whether through employment in the docks, as merchant seamen or serving in the Royal Navy. Henry VIII had created the Royal Docks in 1512 on the slopes of the Thames foreshore, specifically to build his new flagship the *Great Harry*. The illustration from an engraving of around 1854 shows horses being shipped out from the dockyards in Woolwich on the way to the Crimean War, perhaps the actual mounts of the British cavalry who took part in the Charge of the Light Brigade. By the 1860s Greenwich Marsh including the Royal Dockyards at Woolwich was the biggest ship-building area in the world.

A map of Greenwich, 1869. The Greenwich Hospital and Royal Naval School are prominent towards the centre of the map. Many of the road and street names are the same as those today, but others have changed since the mid-1900s. At the top right of the map is Marsh Lane, not much more than a track

running into the Greenwich Marsh. This is now a major road, Blackwall Lane, leading to the latest Greenwich regeneration area, with houses, apartments, cinema, restaurants, hotels and sports and leisure complexes.

A site board on a commercial property on Greenwich Marsh, an unusual place to find the famous Meridian Line. Greenwich Marsh once covered the area now known as the Greenwich Peninsular, the present site of the Millennium Dome. As well as ship-building, there were many other industries located within this vast stretch of land, including chemical manufacturing and iron working. In the early times fishing and barging would have been carried out along the shores, as well as some smuggling. Most of the industries closed long ago, and are now being replaced by new housing developments.

Morden College, thought to have been designed by Sir Christopher Wren, was built on the edge of Blackheath to house up to forty single or widowed merchants. A large part of the Greenwich Marsh was once owned by Morden College, a charity founded by Sir John Morden in 1695 to provide homes for merchants who lived in and had businesses in Greenwich, and had fallen on hard times either through accidents or disasters at sea. The estate owned many other properties in the area specifically as rental accommodation for residents and families of Greenwich, my own family being one.

Observatory, Greenwich.

Following the Meridian Line back from the Marsh will bring you to the Royal Observatory, the more famous site on the Meridian Line sitting high upon Greenwich Hill within the park grounds. Sir Christopher Wren designed the original structure specifically for the Astronomer Royal John Flamsteed on instruction from Charles II. The King promised to pay £500 towards the building costs, and included reclaimed material from a demolished gatehouse at the Tower of London and spare bricks from Tilbury Fort. The image shows the Royal Observatory at the turn of the twentieth century before the many additions and alterations to the building.

In 1884 an international delegation decided that a single prime meridian should replace the numerous ones in existence all around the world at that time. It was decided that the line would pass through the principal transit instrument at the Royal Observatory to be the Initial Meridian and all longitude would be calculated from this point. After the Second World War the observatory moved to new premises in Sussex but the building, now a museum, and the Meridian Line remain. A brass strip runs across the forecourt of the Observatory and an adjacent path where you can stand astride the line dividing the east and west of the globe.

A view from the Greenwich Observatory looking down towards the Thames during the Second World War. The historic Royal Naval College and Naval School is the backdrop to an unusual scene of what appears to be a vegetable garden in the park grounds. It was the case during the war that every piece of available land should be used for growing supplies to supplement rationing. Most Greenwich residents would have had a vegetable patch in their garden, and many would keep chickens and rabbits for extra meat. Greenwich and its residents have seen many changes through the years, and if you look out towards the Royal Naval College from the Observatory today, it's the imposing structures of Canary Wharf that catch the eye.

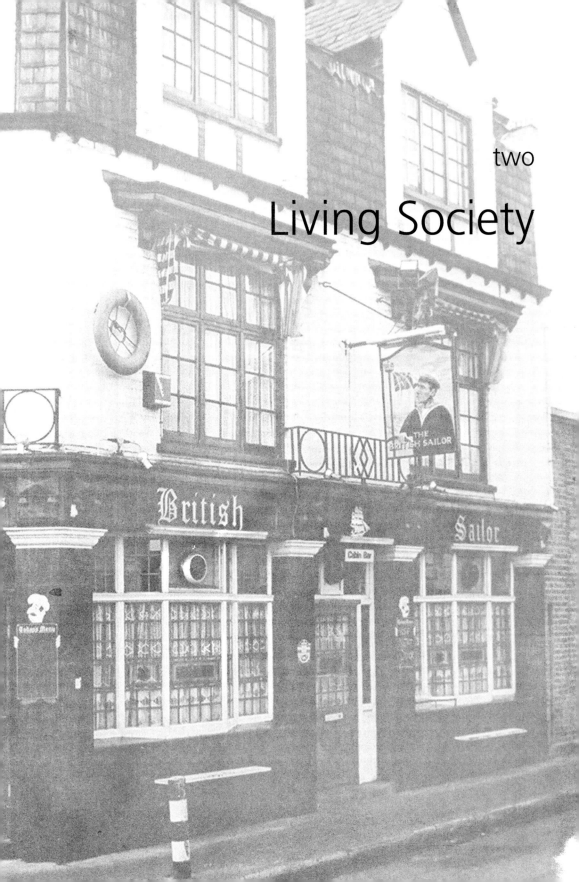

two

Living Society

A society built up on the river had revolved around ships, shipping, water and the wharfs, and the people that were proud of Greenwich and its heritage. Many areas and places in Greenwich grew out of a social need, whether coming by way of building houses, shops, hospitals and almshouses or by providing places of worship, schools, theatres, pubs and dining establishments for MPs.

A North-West View of Greenwich Church.

A group of gentlemen of Greenwich founded the Miller Hospital in 1783 on Greenwich Road (now Greenwich High Road) as the Kent Dispensary for the Poor. In 1837 Queen Victoria became the patron. The Revd Canon John Cale Miller, vicar of St Alphege was a major fundraiser for the dispensary. After his death in 1880 the dispensary was enlarged and renamed the Miller Hospital in 1908. Originally one of the first public hospitals in Greenwich, it was considered too costly to modernise, and was closed and then demolished in 1975.

Opposite: Greenwich church, or St Alphege's, is the main place of worship in Greenwich. The present church was built on the site of a much earlier building erected as a memorial to Alphege, Archbishop of Canterbury, who was killed on the spot in 1012. Taken hostage by the Danes, he was brought to Greenwich and held to ransom. When he refused to let himself be traded for a ransom he was stoned to death by his captors. The church was rebuilt in the thirteenth century, and it was here that Henry VIII was baptised. Parts of the church were rebuilt after a storm, and again after extensive bomb damage during the war.

A panoramic view of the Royal Naval College and Maritime Museum at the turn of the twentieth century. The original college building, started in 1664, was intended to be the new Palace of Placenta for King Charles II but was never finished. In 1692 Queen Mary ordered that on its completion it should provide a Naval Hospital with architects Wren and Hawksmoor working on the new design. In 1873 The Royal Naval College moved from Portsmouth to occupy the site. The National Maritime Museum buildings, part of which were originally intended as a palace for King James I's consort Anne of Denmark, were used as a royal residence. They then became the Greenwich Park Rangers house until 1806 when the Naval School moved in. The Maritime Museum took over the property, opening to the public in 1937.

Opposite above: Greenwich Pensioners drinking outside an inn near the Greenwich Hospital in the late 1700s from a sketch by Isaac Cruickshank, a celebrated artist depicting social life of the time. The pensioners, whose numbers were reaching almost 3,000 by 1814, had a large staff headed by an admiral to care for their needs. The hospital had a bakery, brewery and infirmary. All the residents were provided with uniforms and tobacco and could carry out simple duties to earn money which they no doubt spent in the local inns.

Opposite below: Naval Heroes. The painting shows some of the hospital's residents from the mid-1800s commemorating the Battle of Trafalgar in Greenwich Park. The hospital, established as a residential home for injured sailors and seafarers, was based along the same lines as Chelsea Hospital. Many veterans of Trafalgar were residents at the Greenwich Hospital.

William Gladstone addresses a crowd on Blackheath in 1876 with regard to the Turkish atrocities being carried out in Bulgaria. One-time Conservative, then Liberal MP, Gladstone became Prime Minister in 1886. He was one of many Parliamentarians to visit Greenwich for government business and pleasure.

Opposite above: Seat of local power during the 1930s was the Council Chambers in the Old Town Hall, West Greenwich. Greenwich was once a metropolitan borough which amalgamated with the Borough of Woolwich to form the London Borough of Greenwich in 1965. The Council Chambers then transferred to Woolwich Town Hall. At the very top of the picture you can just make out the lower part of the original crest of Greenwich Borough.

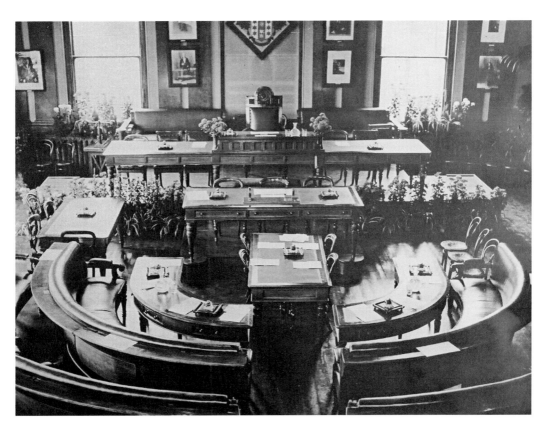

The Ship Tavern, a famous public house at the turn of the twentieth century, was situated just west of the Naval College on the present site of the clipper ship the *Cutty Sark*. The inn would have been frequented by Naval personnel, merchant seamen and Greenwich residents alike during this time and was a favourite dining place for Conservative MPs who came there to sample its renowned whitebait suppers.

The Trafalgar Hotel,

PARK ROW, : : : : : : GREENWICH.

☛ *TURN SHARP TO LEFT COMING OFF PIER.* ☚

LARGE
BANQUETING
ROOMS.

PUBLIC AND
PRIVATE
DINING ROOMS.

BEDROOMS.

BILLIARDS.

GARAGE.

WEDDING
RECEPTIONS
A SPECIALITY.

SPACIOUS
BALL ROOM.

WINES,
SPIRITS,
LIQUEURS.

MODERATE
TARIFF.

F. SHARP, Photo.   By special appointment to the Admiralty.   27, Trafalgar Rd., Greenwich, S.E.

SPECIAL FISH DINNERS TO ORDER AT SHORT NOTICE.

ALL ROOMS OVERLOOK RIVER.

Telephone: NEW CROSS 413.   G. DAMIRAL, Proprietor.

Rear of the Trafalgar Tavern showing the building before one of its many refurbishments. The signage on the wall gives a somewhat bleak message to those seeking work in the area.

Opposite above: The Ship Tavern was one of the largest inns to be found in Greenwich; during its heyday it would be filled with people travelling down from London to enjoy ale by the river or a meal in the restaurant. Dickens dined here with his literary friends. It is thought to be the place that, in 1857 while dining with Dickens, Douglas Jerrold, London playwright and one of the founders of *Punch Magazine*, was taken ill before dying just a few days later. Jerrold had himself been in the Navy, joining as a boy sailor at just ten years of age. The building was demolished after bomb damage during the war.

Opposite below: Advertisement for the Trafalgar Tavern from the mid-1900s. In the Victorian period the Conservatives favoured the Ship Tavern whilst the Liberals would journey down river to supper at the Trafalgar Tavern. Built in 1837 for Greenwich Hospital the tavern replaced the older George Inn. Frequently used for banquets and functions as shown in this advertisement, Charles Dickens, who was also regular visitor at the Trafalgar, set the wedding breakfast from his novel *Our Mutual Friend* at the tavern.

A rather unusual image of the *Cutty Sark*. This world-famous clipper ship was moored in dry dock in 1954 and it took almost three years before she was re-rigged and ready for opening to the public. Built on the Clyde in 1889, she sailed the world trade routes for nearly fifty years. This wonderful ship attracts hundreds of thousands of visitors a year from all around the world and is currently undergoing total restoration with half of the estimated £25 million renovation costs coming from the Heritage Lottery Fund.

Opposite above: A Sunday school outing from 1922 where children pose in front of a charabanc outside the Trafalgar Tavern. These long open-topped buses were a popular mode of transport for trips into the countryside or if lucky, a day out to the seaside. Holidays would have been a luxury for working-class people from Greenwich at the turn of the century and organised works outings and school trips were their only chance of getting some well-earned relaxation.

Opposite below: Crane Street during the 1800s is not much more than an alleyway running behind the Trafalgar Tavern and along to Highbridge Wharf. A crane to unload ships had stood there from at least 1730. A row of terraced houses are seen on the right of the street, with the Yacht public house positioned about halfway along on the left. The Yacht's age is unknown, but there had been a river pub here for at least 300 years. In the eighteenth century it was called the Barley Mow.

At the end of Crane Street, next to a set of gates that lead down to the river stood the Three Crowns, one of the smaller riverside inns. This picture shows a group of local residents in 1937 gathered around some street sellers at the top of East Street.

Opposite above: The Three Crowns from Thames side in the late 1900s. If the public house were here today it would have been Listed and protected from destruction. But it was one of many riverside pubs lost to the continued development along the river frontage.

Opposite below: In the foreground of this picture from 1919 is the weather-boarded building that once housed the headquarters of the Curlew Rowing Club, reputedly the oldest rowing club on the tideway. The Crown & Sceptre, later to become a conservative club before being demolished in 1934, is just to the right. Both buildings once stood on what is now Highbridge Wharf. It is the probably site of a fifteenth-century 'bridge', linking the wharf to ships and boats loading and unloading goods and passengers. This was also a point on the Thames beyond which Venetian galleys were forbidden to proceed upstream as decreed by Venetian Senate in 1453.

The Three Crow

The Crowley family at one time owned Anchor Wharf, a short walk down river from the Naval College. Sir Ambrose Crowley, a Newcastle iron founder, owned the house depicted to the left of the illustration. Originally built in 1647, the splendid residence was referred to by the locals as the 'old palace', and was thought at the time to have been Elizabethan. Demolished in 1854, Greenwich Power Station, originally built to power the tram system, now occupies the site. It was said that the house grounds, when cleared, were found to be scattered with anchors made by the Crowley Co.

Opposite above: Somewhat dwarfed by a huge power station that stands next door, Trinity House, founded in 1613 by Henry Howard, Earl of Northampton, was built as an almshouse to provide charitable accommodation for twenty old men of good character. Later, married couples were allowed to occupy some of the larger accommodation. Trinity House, depicted during the early 1800s, was restored in 1812 and the building is thought to be the oldest in Greenwich.

Opposite below: One of the last Greenwich riverside public houses to come under the developers' hammer was the British Sailor, demolished to make way for modern luxury riverside apartments at the beginning of the Millennium. It was close to here that merchant ships from eastern block countries would tie up in the 1960s, their crews trading vodka for English cigarettes with the locals, myself being one.

The Cutty Sark Tavern on Ballast Quay, late 1950s. Built in the early 1800s, the public house sits in a row of terraced houses called Union Place. Once called the Union Tavern, it was renamed when the *Cutty Sark* became a permanent fixture in Greenwich. Ballast Quay, a name dating back nearly 400 years, was where ships came after offloading their cargo to load ballast dug out from local gravel pits for their return trips home.

Opposite above: Stables at the back of Prospect Place with Greenwich Power Station just visible in the background, early 1900s. Up until the 1960s it was still possible to find the odd working stable hidden away at the rear of a building or end of a cul-de-sac.

Opposite below: Trafalgar Road at the turn of the nineteenth century filled with rows of retail shops, pubs and coffee houses. You could purchase anything you needed right on your doorstep. In the picture you can see one of Greenwich's early modes of public transport – a horse-drawn tram.

GREENWICH
BATHS & WASH-HOUSES.

This Establishment is now open to the Public for BATHING from Eight o'clock in the morning until Eight at night, and on Saturdays until Ten at night. On Sundays, from Eight until Nine in the morning only.

From April 1st to October 31st, it opens at Six every morning, and closes at Nine at night, except Saturdays, when it is open until Ten o'clock. On Sundays, from Six until Eight in the morning only.

1st CLASS—Entrance in London-street.	2nd CLASS—Entrance in Royal-hill.
WARM .... 6d.	WARM.......................... 2d.
COLD.......................... 3d.	COLD .... 1d.
VAPOUR BATH 6d. SHOWER BATH 3d.	VAPOUR BATH 2d. SHOWER BATH 1d.
N.B. Each bath is in a separate room; every bather has clean water, and two clean towels.	N.B. Each bath is in a separate room; every bather has clean water, and one clean towel.

For several Children, not exceeding Four, under Eight years of age, including the use of one clean towel for every child.

FIRST CLASS—WARM......... 6d.	SECOND CLASS—WARM ...... 4d.
COLD .... 3d.	COLD....... 2d.

There are Separate Entrances to the Men's and Women's Baths.

THE TEPID PLUNGING BATHS.

Open on the same days and during the same hours as above.

1st CLASS—Entrance in London-street.	2nd CLASS—Entrance in Royal-hill.
EACH BATHER.................. 4d.	EACH BATHER .... 2d.

WASHING, DRYING, AND IRONING DEPARTMENT.

Open from 8 o'Clock in the Morning until 5 in the Afternon (Sundays excepted).
Entrance in Royal Hill.

FOR THE FIRST HOUR.. 1d.——FOR EVERY SUCCEEDING HALF-HOUR.. 1d.

N.B. Each Woman Washing has a place to herself, with as much clean water (hot and cold) as she requires, and steam for boiling the linen, a separate horse for drying the clothes, with the convenience of ironing, and the use of irons and ironing blankets.

The Commissioners issue

ANNUAL TICKETS,

Not transferable, entitling the holder to bathe in any part of the Establishment during twelve months from the date of issue, for ONE GUINEA.

Arrangements have been made for the accommodation of persons desiring to take

LESSONS IN SWIMMING.

For Terms apply to the Superintendent, at the Establishment.

The Commissioners having determined to allow ADVERTISEMENTS to be placed in the Waiting-rooms, and in other parts of the Building, have fixed the Prices as follow, subject to the regulations under-stated :—

A Single Advertisement .. per Ann. £1 1 0	Three Advertisements .. per Ann. £1 16 0
Two do. .. ,, 1 10 0	Four do. .. ,, 2 2 0

And for every additional Advertisement, a further sum of 10s. 6d. per annum.
No Advertiser to be allowed to place more than one Advertisement on the same subject in any one Room.

Each Advertisement must be framed according to a pattern approved by the Commissioners; the expense of which Frame, as well as all expenses attending hanging the same, to be paid by the parties advertising.
By order of the Commissioners,
E. W. JAMES, *Clerk.*

An advertisement from the 1900s for the local bathhouse in London Street (now Greenwich High Road) announcing it is now open for bathers with first- and second-class amenities. Most of the working-class people of Greenwich would not have had their own indoor bathing facilities so bathhouses like these were commonplace within the area.

Opposite above: A typical high street grocer's shop from the early 1900s you would think, but Lipton's in Trafalgar Road is displaying the Royal Coat of Arms and is proudly proclaiming they are trading 'By Special Appointment to His Royal Majesty the King'.

Opposite below: Tenants of Tusker Street celebrate outside their homes during the early 1900s. These houses are typical of the type of terraced properties found throughout Greenwich where the working class would have lived. Most of East and Lower Greenwich had row upon row of Victorian and Edwardian two-up, two-down properties occupied by tenants who worked within the local trades and industries.

The wealthier residents of Greenwich would live in the larger family homes in Blackheath and West Greenwich. This family group photograph from the 1920s shows a property in Vanbrugh Fields just off Maze Hill. It looks rather palatial compared to the working-class terraced housing found not too far away on the Greenwich 'lower road'.

Opposite above: At the junction of Trafalgar Road and Vanbrugh Hill once stood the large imposing Union Workhouse. Erected in 1840, it served as a place of refuge for the poor of Greenwich who had no means to support themselves. Over 1,000 inmates could be accommodated where they earned their keep by working at picking oakum, winding silk and spinning jerseys. The rooms were occupied by various class of inmates, including rooms for 'bad women'.

The workhouse became an infirmary, and was then converted into a hospital, St Alphege. This large Victorian institution, seen here shortly before it was demolished in the 1960s, made way for a new hospital, a concrete monstrosity considered state of the art in its time. This building was closed down towards the end of the 1900s, and has now also been demolished to make way for a new modern housing and leisure complex.

Above: A publicity leaflet from the 1860s handwritten by the landlord of the Ship & Billet public house, stables and tearooms. Positioned opposite the workhouse on the corner of Marsh Lane (now Blackwall Lane) that was nothing more than a narrow track running down to the Greenwich Marshes. The pub is still there but has changed somewhat from the one in this illustration.

Opposite above: Buildings on Trafalgar Road during the mid-1900s. Known locally as the 'lower road', due to the fact it was positioned at the base of the hills that stretched up to Blackheath and beyond, the road was named after Nelson's victory at Trafalgar. Over the years the early Victorian properties were gradually demolished and replaced by more modern, uninteresting shops and offices. Some of the original buildings were refurbished and modernised and can still be spotted hiding behind a façade of modern shop fronts and signage.

Opposite below: By the early 1900s most of Greenwich Marsh had been developed, and the workers from the industries that had spread across the marshland had formed their own communities with shops, pubs, schools and a church. One of the community groups from the Blakey workers' homes are seen here setting off on an outing to Dymchuch to celebrate King George VI's coronation in 1937. As the industries declined so did the communities and almost all of the original houses and buildings have now been demolished.

The Sea Witch just before the Second World War, a communal meeting place for the workers on the west shore of the peninsular. The pub was situated overlooking the Thames on the Marsh Wall where the Tunnel Glucose site is today. It was here that Thames lightermen would sign on for work. During the war the area was a prime target for German bombing raids, and one night in 1940 the pub was hit and destroyed. The only original public house left on the peninsular is the Pilot Inn built in 1801.

three

Industrious
People

For several hundred years Greenwich and the surrounding areas were a centre of industry, recreation and tourism. By the late 1800s the Industrial Revolution had transformed manufacturing, ship-building, engineering and construction throughout the country. The one time Green Harbour on the river was now becoming one of London's biggest areas of commercial growth and employment.

LAUNCH OF THE LADY DERBY AT MESSRS. MAUDSLAY'S BUILDING-YARD, EAST GREENWICH.

Above: Ships and ship-building is part of Greenwich history, from the time of the Tudors to the reign of George V. Greenwich Marsh was one of the biggest ship-building areas in Europe. Henry Maudslay, born in Woolwich in 1771 and working as a powder monkey in the Royal Arsenal as a boy, became one of the finest precision engineering manufacturers of his age. Maudslay had a shipyard at Bay Wharf where many fine ships were built and launched such as the *Lady Derby* in 1865. Clipper ship *Blackadder* and her twin *Halloween* were built here in 1870. A piece of equipment much smaller than a ship but very important to shipping was also constructed here, the time ball on the top of Flamsteed House at the Greenwich Observatory, one of the world's earliest time signals for shipping on the Thames.

Opposite above: Whether building, sailing or unloading ships there was always work to be found on the river for the people of Greenwich. At the turn of the twentieth century steam was starting to overtake sail but there were still plenty of sailing ships working the river Thames, coastal waters and beyond. The *Sarah Amy*, a barquetine launched in 1871, is seen tied up alongside Huntley's Wharf close to the Trafalgar Tavern; a few of the crew are looking out from her deck. She was a typical sailship of that period. Some full-rigged ships were converted during this time into barquentines or barques as they would be much easier to handle on the open sea.

One of Greenwich's most famous ships, the
Cutty Sark was converted from a full-rigged
sailing ship into a barquentine shortly after
the First World War. When badly damaged in
a storm, her Portuguese owners at that time
decided to save some money by refitting her
as a barquentine. Wilfred Dowman, a retired
sailing ship captain, saw the *Cutty Sark* in
Falmouth Harbour and became determined
to buy the ship and restore her to her former
glory. In 1923 his dream came true, and this
painting from that year depicts her moored
in the Surry Docks, fully restored. Thirty
years later the *Cutty Sark* would be placed in
dry dock at Greenwich as a monument to
those bygone days.

THE " CUTTY SARK " IN THE SURREY DOCKS

52

Above: The *Dreadnought*, moored off Greenwich, was the last of three hulks used as hospital ships for sick and injured seamen. The first, *Grampus*, was loaned by the Admiralty in 1821. This was replaced by the larger *Dreadnought* in 1831 and then by the much bigger 120-gun *Caledonia*, renamed *Dreadnought*. The ship built during the Napoleonic War, once the flagship of Admiral Pellew, was eventually abandoned and broken up in 1872 when the last patients were transferred to the shore-based infirmary.

Opposite above: Crew members of the *Cutty Sark* from her heyday during the late 1800s. There were plenty of men from Greenwich who took to the seas during these times, either as merchant sailors working on sailing ships and steamers or as recruits from the Cadet School serving in the Royal Navy. Even today you will find a crew on the *Cutty Sark* ready and willing to welcome you aboard the only original tea clipper ship in existence.

Opposite below: Royal Naval College staff line up for a very large group photograph. Originally the site was occupied by The Greenwich Hospital. In 1869 the hospital closed, and the Royal Naval College took the buildings over for use as a naval training centre for officers. In 1919 the Naval Staff College was opened on the site, and during the war almost 27,000 Naval personnel were trained at Greenwich. The Navy moved out in 1998.

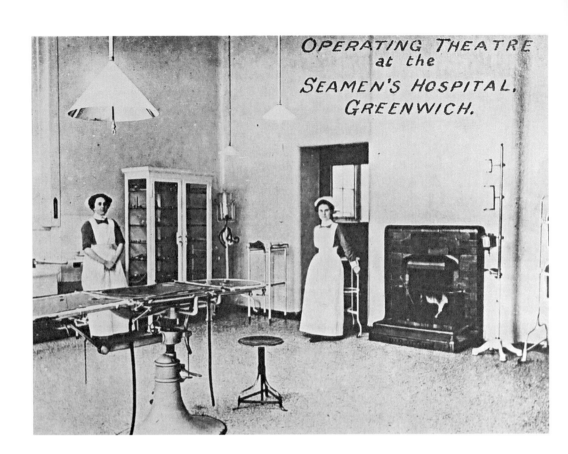

OPERATING THEATRE at the SEAMEN'S HOSPITAL, GREENWICH.

Above: Billingsgate Dock during the early 1800s. Once the base of a North Sea fishing fleet with a history going back to the fourteenth century, smacks from Greenwich were sailing north well into the mid-1800s. Many young men from Greenwich worked on these boats as apprentices, a very dangerous but profitable trade. When steam began to replace sail, the Greenwich-based fleet relocated to Grimsby. The dock was near the entrance of the Greenwich foot tunnel, but nothing now remains of this very ancient port.

Opposite above: Medical theatre in the Dreadnought Seamen's Hospital, previously the infirmary of the main hospital built between 1764 and 1786. Damaged after a fire in 1811, the infirmary was extensively rebuilt with more alterations carried out during the 1840s. When the main hospital closed, the Seamen's Hospital Society leased the infirmary from the Admiralty to administer medical and surgical care of sick and injured merchant seamen.

Opposite below: Patient arriving by a motor ambulance used by the Seamen's Hospital Society in the early 1900s. During the late nineteenth and early twentieth centuries, the generosity of the society allowed the hospital to treat urgent medical cases involving local residents from Greenwich, Deptford and Blackheath as well as merchant seamen. The hospital became part of the NHS and, as with a majority of other smaller localised hospitals, was eventually closed down in 1986. The buildings still remain as part of Greenwich University.

PETER BOATS AT GREENWICH.

Above: Peter boats at Greenwich in 1828. These popular Thames clinker-built row and sailboats were used to catch fish below and above London Bridge with different types used depending on what part of the river was fished (above or below bridge). Each boat had a small hold amidships for storing their fresh catch. During this time the Thames was full of young sprat and herring and local fishermen would have a ready market selling to many of the riverside inns such as the Ship Tavern and Trafalgar Tavern at Greenwich. Salmon was also very abundant and cheap; in fact people were getting tired of eating it.

Left: Shore fisherman on his way to market during the 1800s with a basket of freshly caught fish or eels. In the background is Greenwich Hospital. Close by would have been Fisher Lane, running close to the perimeter of the hospital and Greenwich Church Street – a fish market had been here since the late 1600s. The development of Greenwich Hospital and surrounding area saw the end of the market and destroyed nearly all of what was left of streets from medieval times.

NORWAY
SUFFERANCE LANDING WHARF,
THAMES STREET, GREENWICH.

This Wharf is eligibly situated for Landing and Shipping Goods and Machinery of all descriptions, having Powerful Shears and Cranes, capable of lifting, in one piece, 50 Tons, with good depth of Water and easy access; also, a

DRAWING DOCK, WITH EASY INCLINE.

DEPÔT FOR CAEN STONE OF THE FINEST QUALITY,

Imported from Allemagne, Normandy, and Shipped direct to order.

PORTLAND AND ALL DESCRIPTIONS OF YORKSHIRE STONES.

GOODS OF ALL DESCRIPTIONS LANDED, HOUSED, AND CARTED.

c c

An advertisement for Norway Wharf from the late 1800s promoting the heavy-lifting gear for unloading stone and timber imported from Northern Europe. The wharfs on the Greenwich river frontage stretched from Deptford Creek to the Greenwich Marshes, employing hundreds of local workers from the area. Generations of families would have worked on the Thames as watermen and lightermen. An Act of Parliament in 1555 had established the Company of Watermen & Lightermen who were responsible for the movement of goods and passengers on the river Thames.

The big freeze of 1895. Huge ice flows were created on the Thames when a prolonged cold spell in February of that year brought river traffic and work on the river to a virtual standstill. Barges and lighters from Greenwich and most other stretches of the Thames were immobilised being frozen in by the ice. Any steamers that could navigate the river were unable to be loaded or unloaded so the whole river industry suffered. This had a knock-on effect for all other businesses that relied on the river trade.

Below: To the west of Greenwich runs Deptford Creek, physically dividing Greenwich and neighbouring Deptford. It was to the west of Deptford Creek where Henry VIII established the Royal Naval Dockyards in 1593 and the once small fishing village expanded into a busy dockyard town. The creek was not crossed by a permanent structure until 1815. The river Ravensbourne flowing into the Thames at Deptford Creek is one of the few remaining navigational creeks on the Thames, depicted here during the 1950s. Developments in the area included the East India Co.'s ship-building yard, corn tide mills (there since the twelfth century), the king's slaughter house, wood sawmills, chemical works and a variety of potteries and tanneries. With the loss of the Royal Dockyard in the mid-1800s the area has been going through continued change and regeneration.

John Penn Senior founded Penn's Ironworks located off Blackheath Road in 1799. The company expanded into marine engine manufacture when his son took over the works in 1843 after which it was reputed to have been the biggest marine engine builders in the world. The company started by making engines for a number of boats working between Greenwich and London, using the superior oscillating type of engines rather than the side lever principle. The Royal Navy commissioned the company to supply engines for Naval vessels including HMS *Warrior, Black Eagle, Sphynx, Banshee* and the Royal Yacht *Victoria & Albert*. The Thames Ironworks eventually acquired the company in 1899, the company that built several of the early *Dreadnought* battleships at Blackwall. Nothing of the Penn site remains apart from John Penn Road located south of Blackheath Road.

Mumford's Flour Mill was situated on the south side of Deptford Creek, established on the site since 1790 and originally a wooden building powered by the tides. The building shown from around the late 1800s is a later brick-built structure. The corn that was turned into flour at the mill was brought up river by barge. The grain-milling industry went through a period of radical change during the late 1800s when new technology not only affected employment but the location of mills in general; the traditional milling with stones using natural power was replaced by steam-powered milling with rollers.

A GRAIN SILO AT GREENWICH · Mr Aston Webb, F.R.I.B.A., Architect

An architect's drawing of the elegantly designed grain silo at
Mumford's Flour Mill built during 1897. The silo was a huge
structure and used the most modern design specifications
of the time including internal metal framing and the latest
fireproof building technology. The mill buildings were still
owned by the Mumford family until the 1960s when they
were sold. The remaining mill buildings are now Listed and
have been turned into luxury apartments.

At least three mills were erected on Blackheath during the 1700s, typical of the type found throughout London at that time. Mostly used to grind corn into flour, one mill on Blackheath was used to turn a wood lathe. The high location of the heath made it an ideal spot to erect windmills but they were made redundant by the latest mechanised and much larger mills being developed by Victorian industrialists such as Mumford's Mill at Deptford Creek. The stump of one Blackheath mill remained until the 1850s with all mill sites eventually being built on.

Above: An early Victorian fire appliance manufactured by Merryweather & Sons, one of the leading designers and manufacturers of fire engines throughout the nineteenth and twentieth centuries. The workshop, located in Greenwich High Road, employed many local workers in the production of all types of steam-powered firefighting apparatus including the early hand-pushed appliances, horse-drawn fire engines, self-propelled motorised engines and steam-powered fire boats. The business was still in existence up until the 1960s and the front of the engineering company's works could still be seen in Greenwich High Road. With the continued regeneration of the area there is no guarantee how long it will remain.

Above: A Greenwich Fire Brigade unit out on manoeuvres near Greenwich High Road during the late 1800s. Look high up at some of the older properties in Greenwich and you might see a decorative lead plaque fixed to the wall. They are a legacy from the Great Fire of London in 1666 after which houses would take out insurance to be protected by independent fire brigades – the plaques signified which company the property was insured with.

Opposite below: East Greenwich Fire Brigade at the turn of the nineteenth century with horse-drawn fire appliances that would soon be a thing of the past. The private fire brigades lasted until 1866 when the Metropolitan Fire Brigade was formed. A majority of firemen at the time were ex-sailors earning between £1 to £1 14s a week. In 1904 the Metropolitan Fire Brigade was renamed the London Fire Brigade and motorised vehicles start to replace the previous horse-drawn appliances. The East Greenwich station has now moved to a new building but the old building still remains and has been turned into a hotel.

During the war years a majority of London docklands, including many of the industrial areas around Greenwich, would be ablaze at night due to the continued bombing raids being carried out by the Luftwaffe. The Government passed an Act setting up an auxiliary fire service to work alongside the regular fire brigade, and here they are practicing their firefighting skills up river from the Royal Naval College.

In 1877 Maj.-Gen. P.J. Bainbrigge opened a workshop for the blind of Kent in London Street (now Greenwich High Road) after receiving a bequest of almost £14,000 from the engineer and amateur astronomer James Nasmyth. By 1887 the workshop employed fifteen blind workers to make basket wear, rope work and fenders for use on Thames river craft, wharves and docks. By 1930 the number had increased to forty-one. When the workshop on Greenwich High Road closed, the workers moved to new premises in Eastney Street.

Workers from W.A. Willson's Mineral Water manufacturers in Eastney Street in 1906 who supplied soft drinks throughout Greenwich, including lemonade, ginger beer and cola. The bottled water market was well established at that time. The benefits of mineral water was recognised by the Victorian entrepreneurs who bottled the waters so people could purchase it instead of visiting a particular spring or well. By the mid-nineteenth century the artificial mineral water market became a lucrative business and in turn led to the development of the soft drinks industry.

A dray from W.A. Willson's Mineral Waters, loaded up with soft drinks including a product called Willson's Horehound. Bottled drinks would be sold off the back of the dray to buyers in the street as well as supplying markets, shops and public houses.

An advertisement from a nineteenth-century gazette for Henry Roberts & Co., confectioners in London Street (now Greenwich High Road). For 2d you could buy 1oz of Roberts's infallible cough drops or for 1s you could purchase 1lb of Everton toffee. A line on the advert reads, 'The Confectionary, if pure, may be given to children freely, not only without injury, but with a positive benefit'.

Opposite above: Victorian bottles and cask from Greenwich's own brewer, Lovibonds. The premises were close to the present Greenwich Station on Greenwich High Road where beer would be bottled and casked and delivered to public houses throughout the area. The traditional English ales were once brewed without hops, and then when hops from the continent were introduced beer drinkers developed a taste for the hopped ales. Some of the Victorian beers included porter, stout, bitter and India Pale Ale. A nine-gallon cask of beer cost around 10s 6d.

Opposite below: Works' outing for brewery employees during the late 1800s. These works' outings would normally be organised by the works' foreman, with costs coming from a club fund where employees paid in a few pence on a regular basis. Local transport was hired, sandwiches were packed and bottles of beer stowed. The workers and their families, dressed in their finery, would set off on a simple trip to the country, a fair, a military display or even to see the exhibits at a freak show.

Greenwich Market during the 1800s with a fishmonger and greengrocer on one side and a butcher on the other – the lane between leads to the main covered market square. Greenwich has had several markets in the area for at least 1,000 years; in 1700 a charter was granted after residents campaigned to have a permanent market in the town. The market was held on open ground near to where the *Cutty Sark* is today. It became one of the busiest markets in London, selling fish, vegetables, meat, poultry, live sheep, cattle and horses. The present site was bought in 1831 and a new covered market erected with shops, a slaughterhouse, stables, public houses and even a small music hall theatre.

Opposite above: The market was awarded a Royal Charter in 1849 and should have safeguarded the market's future. A new roof was built to replace the old wooden construction and new shops added, but the crowds and stallholders began to fall away especially after horse-drawn traffic became a thing of the past. Most of the market area was demolished in 1958 and replaced with a new, more modern interior although the historic main entrance was retained. Today the market is as vibrant as it ever was, with arts and crafts, restaurants and wine bars replacing the market stalls of old. However, a threat still hangs over its existence through continued redevelopment of the area.

Before mechanised transport the only way to carry goods was by horse and cart. A majority of larger businesses during the early 1800s would have their own stables, horses, carts and livery staff. This dray is owned by Maltsters Corder & Haycraft, a well-established family-owned business in Greenwich with premises at Hope's Wharf.

Above: For hundreds of years Greenwich has gone through continued change and redevelopment. Buildings have been erected, altered, enlarged, knocked down and then rebuilt. This picture shows workers from around the late 1800s demolishing a section of property in King William Walk. During this time, labourers would earn around 20s a week, no doubt some of which would be spent in the Kings Arms public house to the right of the picture. Known by locals as the 'bunker bar', several stories have circulated to how it acquired the name. Most refer to a time during the Blitz when patrons would go to a makeshift bar 'bunker' downstairs to carry on drinking throughout the air raids.

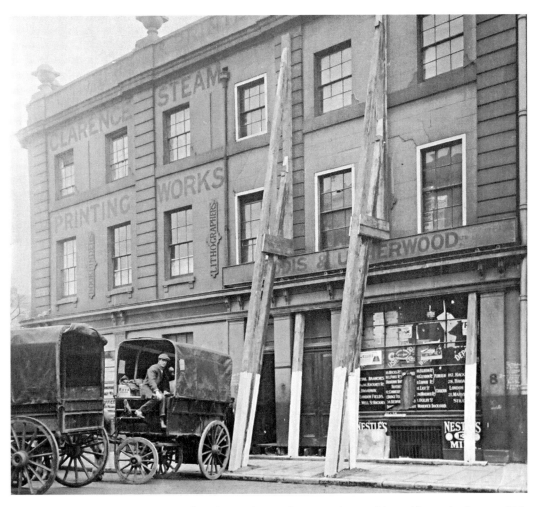

Shops and printing works in College Approach seem in a precarious position with wooden braces which appear to be holding up the front of the building during the early 1900s. The printing works and grocers are long gone but there are still shops in the row, mostly selling antiques, antiquarian books and prints, even apartments, flats and houses. At the time of writing a three-bedroomed house in College Approach costs just over half a million pounds – in the early 1900s it would probably have been around £500.

Opposite below: Walking up the slight incline of King William Walk you come to the road entrance of Greenwich Park and on the left the statue of King William IV himself. Labourers are erecting the statue on the site of St Mary's church during 1936. The statue had originally stood on King William Street near London Bridge – due to street widening it was removed and found a new home in Greenwich. The King was a friend of Lord Nelson whom he met while serving in the Royal Navy, and gave away the bride at Nelson's wedding. William became King on the death of his brother, George IV, in 1830.

A bill of receipt from the 1850s for Teesdale's Furniture Warehouse on Church Street, Greenwich. If you were a wealthy Victorian looking for a fashionable place of residence in Greenwich, Teesdale Furniture Warehouse could completely furnish your new home – supplying bedsteads, dining tables, chairs, sofas and wardrobes to floor rugs, blankets and quilts.

Opposite above: In the thriving Greenwich community there were plenty of shops selling goods of all kinds. At the turn of the twentieth century, a row of shops in Greenwich High Road which were all owned by one merchant shows a variety of wares on display including sandwiches, cooked meats, joints of meat, vegetables, wines, spirits and beers. The cost of produce would vary depending on availability, such as locally caught fish that was cheap and plentiful. Salmon was around 1s per pound, scallops 6d per dozen, a large leg of mutton 4s 8d and potatoes 1d per lb.

Opposite below: Union Wharf and the Cutty Sark public house in the late 1950s, one of the last areas to fall under the redevelopers' hammer towards the end of the twentieth century. This whole stretch of river frontage from the Royal Naval College to the Greenwich **Marsh** will soon be unrecognisable from the time when the wharfs were a bustling area of employment for the watermen and lightermen of Greenwich. The Cutty Sark public house, originally the Union Tavern, still remains but the cranes, barges, ships, wharfs and warehouses have now gone.

The Harbour Master's office on Ballast Quay is one of the few remaining buildings on the waterfront that reminds people this part of Greenwich was once an important area of industry and shipping on the Thames. The Listed building, erected in 1855, replaced an earlier Harbour Master's office near the Yacht Tavern. The harbour master controlled the movement of colliers, bringing in coal from the North East to supply local industry. The boats would return loaded with ballast, some of which was dug out from gravel pits on Blackheath.

Local transport and motor engineering company P.A. Carter & Son, one of many family businesses that grew up alongside Greenwich's own economic growth. This group of employees from the 1920s are proudly standing outside their yard in Christ Church Way. The office address, presumably in Braddyll Street, is displayed on the gates with a heavy goods vehicle of the day parked outside. The company first used horses and carts to carry loads until motorised vehicles replaced them during the 1900s.

The very first telegraph cable laid across the Atlantic was made in East Greenwich at Glass & Elliot's cable factory. The cable, measuring 2,600 miles in length, was too big to go on any ship other than Brunel's *Great Eastern*. The cable was successfully laid after several attempts in 1886. The site of the works is near to Enderby's Wharf where the telegraph cables were loaded onto the ships. The innovative work carried out on telegraph cable technology makes this one of the most important sites in the history of communications technology. Cable was manufactured on the site until the latter part of the 1900s by STC Submarine Systems Ltd. Alcatel, a telecommunications company, now own the site with the cable manufacturing work being carried out on the continent.

Tar workers on Greenwich Marsh during the early 1900s. Bethel's Tar & Chemical Works employed local labourers and factory workers in the production of material for road construction. By the mid-1900s the area was taken over by the Delta Metal Bronze & Brass Foundry. The South Metropolitan Gas Co. owned much of the land, part of which was occupied by their factory and the Ordinance Wharf Tar Works.

Above: The East Greenwich gasometers were designed by retired industrialist George Livesley. Built in the 1880s, the two gasholders were the biggest in the world and were required to supply the ever-increasing needs of South London. Gas production would be carried out on the huge plant occupying an area where the Millennium Dome stands today and then stored in the gasometers. The weight of the holders sent the stored gas down pipes and into people's homes, street lamps and factories. Changes within the industry and the discovery of North Sea gas made the site virtually redundant by the 1970s.

Below: Employees from East Greenwich Gasworks during the 1920s. The East Greenwich Gasworks employed around 5,000 workers, one of the biggest employers in south-east London. The workers had formed a union by the end of the 1800s to ensure better rates of pay and working conditions. By the end of the nineteenth century workers at the site would be earning an average of £1 10s a week.

Workers from Siemens queuing up to receive their war rations. Siemens Bros was another of the larger industries in the area. The company, who specialised in the production of telegraphy equipment, opened an electrical and cable factory on the Charlton Woolwich boundary, beside the Thames, in 1863. The site consisted of a factory, mechanical workshop and several stores and was the first factory to be run on electricity. It was here during the Second World War that the pipeline 'Pluto' was developed to supply fuel across the Channel for the Allied invasion forces

Crew of the Woolwich Ferry during the 1900s in front of the loading ramp leading from the shore to the ferry deck. The skipper is pictured in the centre of the group, deckhands each side and engineers at the front. A majority of the crew were made up from Thames watermen, a tradition carried through to modern times. In 2004 Woolwich Ferry Captain, Peter Deeks, who started his career as a Thames waterman before joining the ferry as a deckhand, received the MBE for forty years' service on the ferry.

Coombe Farm towards the end of the nineteenth century was probably the last farm to operate within Greenwich. The land and farm were once owned by Henry VIII and were given to his second wife Anne Boleyn. John Angerstein, wealthy merchant and Lloyd's of London underwriter, purchased the farm and surrounding area to build himself a house called Woodlands to the south of the newly acquired land. The farm was then leased out to a tenant for use as a market garden. The Victorian farm buildings were close to the site of Westcombe Park Station. The land was sold off in the late 1800s to build a new housing estate and the farm buildings were demolished in 1901.

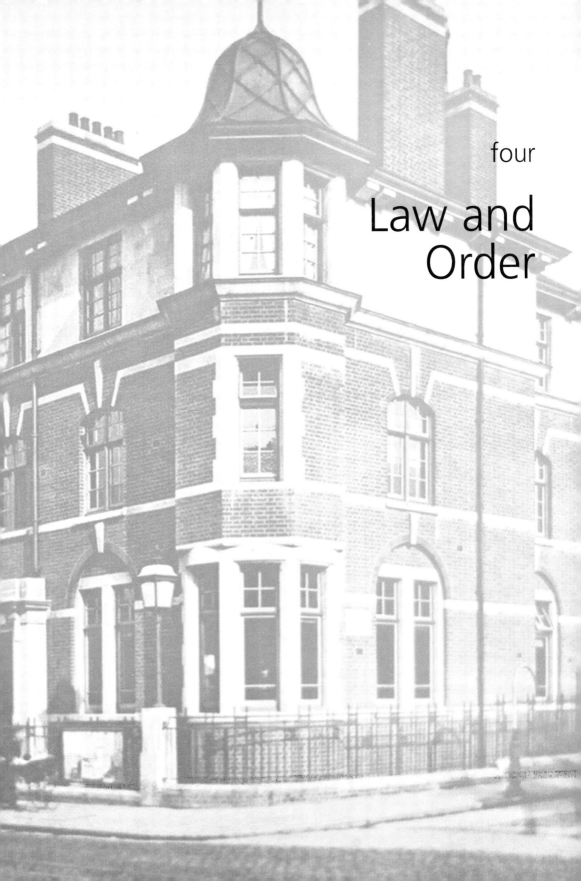

four

Law and
Order

When Victorian crime is mentioned, one case that immediately comes to mind is the Jack the Ripper killings and thoughts of foggy gaslit London streets and alleys with a possible murderer waiting around every corner. This is not a true reflection of crime in London during the late nineteenth and early twentieth centuries. Violent crimes were very unusual. Burglary, pick pocketing, theft and vagrancy were a common occurrence, but assaults and murders were, if not rare, infrequent.

During the latter part of the nineteenth century the Metropolitan Police Force numbered just over 14,000 serving officers with the City of London Police Force totalling almost 1,000. The Metropolitan Police Force were split into divisions signified by a letter. Greenwich or 'R' Division had thirty-eight inspectors, seventy-one sergeants and 476 constables.

On 10 October 1878, at 2 a.m., one of 'R' Division's police constables brought to justice the country's most prolific and cleverest of criminals that the Victorian era had ever seen.

Charlie Peace was a notorious cat burglar, con man, master of disguise and murderer. He was Britain's most wanted man before his capture by local Greenwich PC Edward Robinson.

Greenwich Police Station and Police Court in Blackheath Road in the early 1900s. The first police station in Greenwich was actually sited at the aptly named Cut Throat Lane in 1822 opposite the present Greenwich railway station. It consisted of a simple lock-up cage. The police station at Blackheath Road was operational in 1841 and was rebuilt in 1909. This was the main divisional police station for Greenwich with other localised police stations opening as the force grew in numbers. It was from here that PC Robinson accompanied by PC Girling and Sergeant Brown set off to patrol their beat up on Blackheath, the night Charlie Peace was at large.

Buildings in Park Row, one of which was used as a police station from 1856-1873. Police officers from local stations would patrol the streets in designated beat areas armed with a truncheon and whistle. Although primarily the work of the force was to patrol and safeguard property and persons, they became so efficient at their job that they were called upon to carry out other duties including traffic and crowd control, searching for missing persons and taking 'unfortunates' to hospital for treatment. The police station was said to be haunted by a prisoner who hung himself in one of the cells.

Illustration from a public information leaflet on the methods burglars used to gain entry to property. With Greenwich being one of wealthier areas of London during the nineteenth century, burglars would target the large residential houses on Blackheath and West Greenwich. During 1860 there were 192 recorded burglaries in all metropolitan districts with a value of property taken estimated at £2,852. It was stated at the time that thieves and drunkards caused the greatest problem for the police followed by receivers of stolen goods, prostitutes, vagrants and tramps.

25 Pounds
REWARD.

WHEREAS

On the night of THURSDAY, the 23rd of October, or
early on Friday Morning,

THE PREMISES BELONGING TO

Mr. I. G. Perkins & Mr. Hills,

OF

VANBURGH FIELDS, GREENWICH,

WERE

BROKEN INTO,

AND FROM THE

LARDER

of Mr. PERKINS were stolen, a cut glass blamange dish,
two napkins, and a large sponge. Also the thieves
slaughtered a fine

Doe Deer,

On the premises of Mr. HILLS, which they carried away, and
left a large stick behind them. Whoever may give such information to FARMER and LARKINS, Constables of Greenwich,
as may lead to the apprehension of the person or persons concerned,
shall, upon their commitment, receive half the above reward, and
the other half on conviction, by applying to Mr. PERKINS and
Mr. HILLS as above.

October the 25th, 1828.

HARRIET RICHARDSON, PRINTER, ATLAS PRESS, GREENWICH.

A reward poster from 1828, offering a £25 reward for information
leading to the arrest of thieves who stole items from a larder and
slaughtered a Roe deer, worth at that time around 12s. The reward
seems a relatively large amount for the crime committed but records do
show punishment was severe for certain types of law-breaking. In 1825
a young woman, Ann Clancey, was found guilty of stealing a tobacco
box and gold breast pocket pin from a customer in a Greenwich public
house and was sentenced to seven years transportation. John Broadwood
was found guilty of housebreaking in 1860 and given ten years penal
servitude, while James Higgens, being found in Greenwich and
adjudged a rogue and vagabond, was ordered to be imprisoned and kept
to a day's hard labour.

BARRAUD & JERRARD

PC R20 Edward Robinson joined the Metropolitan Police Force in December 1870 at the age of twenty-two. A local boy, whose family resided in Greenwich, he was a large burly figure, just the right sort for a police officer. His sister, Mrs Sales (my great-great grandmother) ran an unmarried mothers' home in Poplar, East London. PC Robinson was a well-known figure in the community and after apprehending Charles Peace was something of a celebrity. Both PC Robinson and Charlie Peace had waxwork figures made of them by Madame Tussaud, where they were on display until the late 1960s.

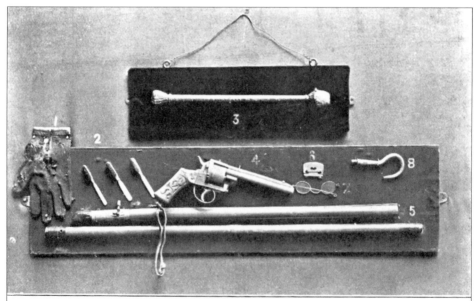

[Geo. H. Wheeler

PEACE'S WEAPONS AND OTHER ARTICLES.

1. Right-hand Glove.
2. Brushes used in dyeing his hair.
3. Life-preserver.
4. Revolver, with strap for attaching to the wrist.

5. Stick (in two sections) which could be used as a violin or as a burglarious implement.
6. Violin-bridge belonging to No. 5.
7. Spectacles.
8. Iron hook which screwed into No. 5, enabling Peace to pull himself up on to a wall or window sill.

(In Madame Tussaud's Exhibition)

Opposite above: It was in the early hours of the morning on 10 October 1878 outside a large house in St John's Park, Blackheath, when PC Robinson saw a light flicker in a downstairs window. The house was typical of the sort of property where a skilful burglar had been carrying out a series of daring house break-ins through out the South East. The burglaries had caused public condemnation and put the police under immense pressure to make an arrest. PC Robinson alerted PC Girling, and then as he climbed over the garden wall he saw Charlie Peace jumping out of a downstairs window. PC Robinson gave chase, and was shot at five times, the last shot going through his arm. Grappling with the man and forcing him down to the ground, PC Robinson held him until PC Girling and Sergeant Brown arrived. Charlie Peace was marched off to Greenwich Police Station while PC Robinson received treatment for his wound.

Opposite below: Charlie Peace's tools-of-the-trade, included brushes for dyeing his hair, a hook and cudgel and the revolver he had used to shoot at PC Robinson. At first the police did not realise they had arrested the notorious Charlie Peace as the wily rouge had been using several false names since moving from the North and taking up residence in Peckham. The image comes from a limited edition publication of the time, handed down through our family.

Below: It was while Peace was being held in Newgate Prison that his identity was revealed by way of the reward offered for information leading to his capture. Peace had been living with his wife and another woman and it was the latter who gave him away to the police. Charlie Peace was wanted for the shooting and murder of Mr Arthur Dyson, husband of a woman he was having an affair with. He had also shot and killed PC Cock in Manchester. At the Old Bailey, Charlie Peace was sentenced to penal servitude for life for the shooting of PC Robinson. Afterwards he was taken back to Yorkshire to stand trail for the murder of Mr Arthur Dyson. Peace made an unsuccessful but daring attempt to escape on the journey back by jumping from the train as depicted in this drawing from the time. He arrived in court and the trial commenced on 4 February 1879 at Leeds Assizes.

THE EXECUTION OF CHARLES PEACE.

Charles Peace was executed on Tuesday morning at Armley Gaol, Leeds, for the murder of Mr. Dyson at Bannercross, near Sheffield, two and a-half years ago. He showed little fear or nervousness, and made, it will be seen, a speech on the scaffold. On Wednesday last he made a confession, which we append, to the Rev. J. H. Littlewood, vicar of Darnall, acknowledging that he had shot Mr. Dyson, as well as a policeman at Manchester, for whose murder a young man named Habron is now undergoing sentence of penal servitude for life. A few minutes before his execution he wrote a letter to his wife, and on the scaffold he made a speech to the reporters. During the night, previous to the execution, he had been visited alternately by the Governor and the Chaplain, and he slept pretty soundly for about four hours before breakfast, of which he partook with apparent relish. About five minutes to eight a procession was formed at the condemned cell, Marwood having previously pinioned the prisoner, who walked to the scaffold with the assistance of two warders. He ascended the scaffold with a slow but steady step, and when placed beneath the cross-beam, he turned to the spectators and gazed intently around him. While the Chaplain was reading the passages from the Burial Service, Marwood tied Peace's feet, and at a pause in the Chaplain's reading, Peace, seeing that Marwood stood ready with the white cap in his hand, turned round and said, "Wait a moment, wait! I must speak." Peace had evidently recognized the four reporters who had been permitted to witness the execution, and in a firm, clear voice he spoke to them as follows: "You gentlemen reporters, I wish you to notice the few words I am going to say. You know what my life has been; that it has been base and bad. I wish to ask the world, after you have seen my death, what man could die as I do if he did not die in the fear of the Lord. Tell all my friends that I feel sure that they have sincerely forgiven me, and that I am going into the Kingdom of Heaven, or else to that place prepared to rest in until the Judgment Day. I have no enemies that I feel to know of on this earth. I wish well to all my enemies, or those who would wish to be so. I wish them well. I wish them to come into the Kingdom of Heaven at last. And now to one and all I say good-bye. Good-bye! Heaven bless you; and may you all come to the Kingdom of Heaven at last. Amen! Say that my last respects are to my children and their dear mother. I hope that no press, no newspaper, will disgrace itself by taunting or jeering them on my account; but have mercy upon them. Oh, God bless you my children! my children each good-bye, and Heaven bless you. Amen" Marwood then drew the white cap over the convict's face, and when that had been done Peace said, "Have you a cup of water you could give me?" No attention was paid to this request, although again was heard from under the cap the words, "May I not have a drink?" and just as the rope was being finally adjusted Peace was heard to exclaim, "Oh, that is too tight." The bolt then almost immediately fell, and in the opinion of the gaol surgeon death must have been instantaneous. When the black flag was hoisted on the principal tower of the gaol there were two or three thousand persons outside the prison walls, a foolish notion having got abroad that even at the last moment the remarkable criminal would cheat the hangman.

Above left: Last photograph of a master criminal, taken around 1879. Found guilty of murder, Charlie Peace was sentenced to death and before execution he confessed to the shooting and murder of PC Nicholas Cock while attempting to burgle a house in Manchester. Charlie Peace was sentenced to hang with the execution taking place in Armley Prison, Leeds on 25 February 1879.

Above right: A newscutting from the period describes Charlie Peace's last few hours in gaol and the final execution. The report gives details of a speech he made from the scaffold and tells how he showed no fear of what was about to happen to him. Over 2,000 people were waiting outside the prison walls as a rumour had circulated that he would attempt to make a dramatic escape, but the crowd were left disappointed.

Above: The first page of a Victorian 'penny dreadful' published in 1879. During his life of crime, Peace had burgled his way around Sheffield and Manchester while posing as a musical instrument salesman. An accomplished violinist, he played in many local concerts and public houses. He made his way south after he had carried out the murders and went to live in Peckham. A well-dressed man, he was small in stature but very strong for his size. He could disguise himself with ease and was renowned for being something of a ladies' man. Charlie Peace was seen as a type of cult hero after his execution, with books and periodicals published about his criminal exploits. Later a film based very loosely on his life was produced and in the 1960s he appeared in a regular strip cartoon of a children's comic.

Opposite above: In 1884 Westcombe Park Police Station opened, replacing the station at Park Row. The police were becoming a larger and more professional force and required more accommodation. In the late 1800s a policeman's basic pay would be around 19s a week, rising to 21s for good conduct – not a tempting salary in those days but good enough for almost 5,000 men to apply to join the force in one year alone. Selection to the force was strict, with only 25 per cent of those applying meeting the required standards and passing the exams.

Opposite below: The grateful residents of St. John's awarded PC Robinson an inscribed silver pocket watch as well as the sum of £25. He was also commended and awarded £25 by the judge at the Central Criminal Court Sessions for courageous conduct. Rewards for police officers during this time seemed commonplace, perhaps to offset poor rates of pay. At the same time PC Robinson received his reward Inspector Abberline received the sum of 40s for actions 'above the call of duty'. Inspector Abberline would go on to be one of the investigating officers in the Jack the Ripper murders.

Below: Things didn't fair so well for PC Robinson. Although serving in the force for another twelve years, he was requested to resign in 1890 due to certain irregularities. It seems he may have taken a drink too often in the local public houses whilst on duty, retelling the story of the night he caught Charlie Peace. After resigning he travelled to Canada and the West Indies in a bid to build a new life, but returned to his birthplace in his late fifties. Working for a while as a night watchman, the last years of his life were spent in the infirmary of the workhouse on the corner of Vanbrugh Hill where he died on 16 May 1926.

A new police station opened in East Greenwich in 1906 on the south side of Park Row at the junction of Trafalgar Road. The building occupied by the old police station in Park Row was bombed in the war and a car park now occupies the area. The East Greenwich Police Station was in use for sixty-four years before its closure in 1962. The building was demolished and new flats erected. The current Greenwich Police Station in Royal Hill was opened when East Greenwich closed. Westcombe Park Police Station has also closed down but is still standing, being designated a Listed building. Blackheath Road Police Station is now Greenwich Magistrates Court.

five

On the Move

When the Danish invasion fleet anchored off Greenwich at the beginning of the ninth century, Greenwich had already become an established riverside community from a time when ancient Britons were laid to rest in burrows overlooking the Thames in what is now Greenwich Park, up to the Romans, who built the road from Kent directly into the heart of Greenwich. The Thames had been the main thoroughfare into London for over 1,000 years, whether used by Roman galley, Viking longship, square rigger or steamboat, but as times moved on so too did means of transport, and the 1800s saw the most dramatic change to the way people travelled.

The Thames had become a major route for all types of shipping but one of the most commonly seen vessels travelling to and fro along the waterway at the turn of the eighteenth century was the Thames barge, seen here during the early 1900s. Barge building was an important trade in Greenwich with one firm, Norton's, based close to the Millennium Echo-Village, surviving until relatively recently. These vessels had evolved from the sea-going sail boat of the Middle Ages and transported and traded goods from London down to the Kent coast and beyond. With the coming of steam, road and railways, these workhorses of the water could have been made redundant. In 1836 an entrepreneur named Mr Henry Dodd founded the annual sailing barge race giving the barges a new lease of life, and they were still being used to transport goods up until the 1970s.

Above: The first London passenger railway, *c.* 1836. Before the early 1800s transport for residents and workers in Greenwich would have been by riverboat, horses or stagecoach. The first London passenger railway opened with a line from Greenwich to London Bridge. Local man Col. George T. Landmann, a retired army officer from Woolwich, designed the railway and although it was an expensive way to travel the service was carrying 2 million people a year by 1844.

Right: Advertising poster from the mid-1800s. The line from Greenwich was built on a viaduct and with 100,000 bricks being laid a day it caused a national brick shortage. The span of the viaduct included 978 arches. The *Royal William* steam locomotive was one of the earliest engines to pull passenger carriages to London and back. On its first journey from London Bridge to Deptford in 1836, it completed the trip in just eight minutes.

LONDON
AND
GREENWICH
RAILWAY.

The Company's Trains run every Quarter of an Hour, from EIGHT in the Morning till ~~QUARTER past EIGHT~~ *NINE* in the Evening, until further Notice.

Fares.——Imperials, 1s.--Mail, 9d.
Omnibus or Open Carriage, 6d.

Free Tickets (not transferable) may be had at the Company's Offices, Cornhill.

Imperials, £5. Mail, £4. Omnibus or Open Carriage, £3. per Qr.

ENTRANCE

Duke Street, foot of **London Bridge,** & **High St. Deptford.**

GEORGE WALTER, *Managing Director.*

MANNING & SMITHSON, Printers, London.

The line from London to Greenwich was expanded with a tunnel dug below Greenwich Park to take a line through to Maze Hill, Charlton, then further out into Kent. In 1888 Greenwich Park Station opened, connecting to a line running from Blackheath and Nunhead. The station was between Stockwell Street and Burney Street, and this picture from 1910 shows the 'sandwich' train with the locomotive in the middle just about to pull away. The line closed in the 1920s.

Steamboat arriving at Greenwich towards the end of the 1800s. When Britain's first official Bank Holiday took place on 7 August 1871, hundreds of workers took advantage of the closure of factories and offices for a day out with their friends and family. With steamboats operating trips up and down the river, Greenwich became a popular destination for Londoners. The boats charged between 2d and 6d per passenger and ran a service approximately every twenty minutes.

Horse-drawn tramways were first introduced into Britain by the American entrepreneur George Francis Train in 1860. Soon tramways would be laid down throughout the suburbs of London. The tram shown, on the Greenwich to Westminster route, is waiting outside the Star & Garter public house in Upper Park Street during 1890. The tram links provided the first convenient means of travel for a majority of residents commuting within the local area and beyond. The horse-drawn trams were still being used in the early 1900s, but they would eventually be replaced by the more modern electrified version.

An electric tram making its way down Greenwich Church Street during 1951. The old horse-drawn tram companies were taken over by London County Council who started running electric trams in 1904. Some trams were powered by overhead cables, while others used an underground conduit system. The Greenwich Power Station was built by the LCC in 1906 to provide electricity to run the trams; it now provides back-up power for the London Underground system.

Trafalgar Road in 1952, strangely devoid of traffic compared to today. The No. 36 tram is heading west past Christ church on the left, and the Crown public house on the right. This route was one of the last to run a tram service within London. Over the previous fifty years the trams had hardly changed at all,

now their routes were gradually being taken over by the more modern trolley and motorbuses. In July 1952 the London tram system finally closed down and the last tram rolled into history.

At the end of the track, a tram being towed away at the depot in Charlton during the mid-1950s. The twin silver tram tracks that ran along many of the roads in Greenwich were the last remnants of a bygone age that could still found on some streets right up until the late 1980s. Between 1950 and 1953 at least one tram a day was broken up for scrap or burnt at the yard. Some were salvaged for preservation with a few going to other areas throughout the country that still had a tram system in operation. There were proposals some time ago to bring the tram system back into use.

For some of the more wealthy residents of Greenwich at the turn of the twentieth century public transport was not for them and the motorcar was the best way to travel. Henry Osborn, at the wheel of the car in the late 1980s, was chauffeur for the mill owners of Mumford's near Deptford Creek. The top model automobile of the day would have cost around £45, and had a top speed of 14mph.

An open-topped bus arriving from the direction of Blackheath is ready to pick up passengers from opposite Blackheath Village Station in the early part of the twentieth century. Several types of buses were developed during these early years, from electric and steam to petrol powered.

In 1933 London Transport was formed, and this new organisation decided to convert all tramways to trolleybus routes. After the war all remaining trams were replaced by motorbuses such as the one seen here in Blackwall Lane. By the start of the swinging sixties the modern diesel-powered red Routemaster buses had replaced both trams and trolleybuses.

Train crash at Maze Hill Station. On 4 July 1958 a steam engine moving out from a siding at the station hit the rear carriage of a train travelling on the same line. Onlookers tell how they saw the engine leap into the air as it crashed into the other carriage. At one time Maze Hill station had several sidings and a

large engine shed before the land was sold off for housing. One of the remaining original station ticket offices to the north of the line is now the workshop of the Maze Hill Pottery.

Before tunnels were built below the Thames for foot passengers, horse-drawn carts and motorised vehicles, a ferry had operated between Greenwich and the Isle of Dogs for several hundred years. One of the most important was the horse ferry established in 1812. Then followed a much larger steam ferry on the same site in 1888 to carry vehicles and even train carriages. It was not profitable and was closed down a few years later. But one of the oldest surviving ferry crossings is between Woolwich and North Woolwich, two parts of the parish lying on opposite sides of the river. A ferry had existed on the site since the Middle Ages; the ferry in the picture is a paddle steamer that operated during the early 1900s.

The Woolwich Ferry during the 1950s with private and commercial vehicles loaded on the top deck. The foot passengers travelled on the deck below and could watch the powerful steam engines working by viewing them through a line of glass windows overlooking the engine room. There were several organisations over the years running ferries across this stretch of water, all charging a fee to travel. When Parliament abolished tolls to cross London bridges in 1877 the people of Woolwich complained that they were still paying a fare to cross on the ferry. After a long wait they were successful in getting a free ferry in 1889.

Terminals were built either side of the river to load and off-load passengers and vehicles; this terminal is on the south side of the river. At first the early ferries only carried a few light vehicles and passengers but during the 1950s more heavy vehicles were using the service. New vessels were needed capable of carrying more vehicles, and larger lorries, with new terminals built to take the increase in traffic. In 1963 the old paddle steamers were replaced by three diesel-powered boats which are still in operation today.

Thames tug towing a load down river from Harvey's Steel Works near Charlton during the mid-1900s. Tugs were used for all types of river work and were extremely powerful for their size. There have been tugs working on the Thames since the early 1830s; originally they were coal-fuelled paddle steamers, many of which were built on the Greenwich Marsh.

Illustration from the late 1930s showing several types of river craft operating along the Thames near Greenwich. There was once an abundance of these craft of all shapes and sizes plying their trade in one of the busiest rivers in the world. These included tramp steamers, barges, cable-laying ships, dredgers, liners, tugs, cargo vessels, warships and the occasional submarine. Today the Thames traffic consists mainly of pleasure boats and river buses taking passengers on trips up and down the river – commercial river craft operating out of Greenwich is now a thing of the past.

six

Sporting
Pastimes

Sporting and leisure activities have been major part of the lives of the people of Greenwich for over 1,000 years, from Tudor times when Henry VIII rode across what is now the front lawns of the Maritime Museum in exhibitional jousts, to the modern sporting confrontations of Premier League Football at Charlton Athletic's home ground, The Valley.

Golfers on a putting green at Blackheath towards the end of the 1800s. Blackheath was home to the oldest golf club outside Scotland. The Royal Blackheath Golf Club, founded in 1608, occupied the north-west part of the heath close to the walls of Greenwich Park.

Above: The club's original headquarters were located in the Green Man public house that stood at the top of Blackheath Hill. This engraving shows the public house as it was during the late 1700s. The name Green Man has associations with the horned god Herne and it is reputed that an effigy of the god can be found in Jack Cade's Cavern below the surface of the heath, not far from the pub's location. The Green Man has now been demolished.

Right: A print from a painting of Henry Challender, *c.* 1812. A prominent golfer of the time, he is depicted wearing the 'field marshall's' uniform of the Blackheath Society of Golfers; the two golf clubs in the painting are still in the possession of the club. In 1923 the golf club merged with Eltham Golf Club, moving to the golf course close to the historic Eltham Palace.

Cricket has been played on Blackheath from the very first time leather hit willow. Many local clubs have used the heath to play matches over the years, with Modern Cricket Club changing its name to Blackheath Cricket Club in 1885. The club then moved to share a ground with Blackheath Rugby Club at Rectory Field, near Charlton. The England Cricket team played several matches very near to the Rectory Field during the late 1800s in a place known as Richardson Field, now long gone.

Sportsman wearing whites could also be found outside the 'Rangers House' to the south-west of Blackheath, where energetic Victorians and Edwardians played tennis. Several tennis clubs could be found in the more affluent areas of Greenwich and Blackheath. Today anyone can play tennis on the courts on the heath for a nominal fee.

Rugby football is another of the more established sports within Greenwich, with Blackheath Rugby Club being the oldest open rugby club in the world. The 'Club', as Blackheath Rugby club is known, was formed in 1858 by the Old Boys of Blackheath Preparatory School, and played home matches at Rectory Field near Charlton. This print depicts the 'Club' scoring a try against Cardiff around 1895.

The 'Club' team line up from 1862. One year on and the game of rugby was transformed completely after a meeting at a London inn attended by eleven rugby football clubs. A new set of rules were proposed which excluded hacking and holding the ball. The 'Club' opted out, deciding to carry on the traditions of running with the ball; from then on rugby and football became two separate sports. Blackheath Rugby Club is one of the seven to have survived out of the original twenty who formed the Rugby Union in 1871.

Blackheath, steeped in history, has been a site for leisure and pleasure activities for several hundred years. The ever-popular fairs have been held at Blackheath since 1689 and although at that time the heath was renowned for being frequented by highway men and robbers, hundreds would climb the steep hills from Lower Greenwich to join in the festivities.

Illustration of a fair on Blackheath, *c.* 1931. In the background is Blackheath village and although the heath has a long and ancient history, the village is comparatively new. In the eighteenth century the village consisted of a couple of cottages – the church with more buildings following on by supply and demand.

A Victorian big wheel at a fair on Blackheath, taking pleasure seekers high into the sky for a panoramic view of the area. You will still find fairs and circuses operating on Blackheath during Bank Holidays and summer festivals. Families from Greenwich as well as further afield come to take a ride on the dodgems and carousels or to visit one of the many circuses that make regular appearances on Blackheath, including the Chinese and Moscow State Circuses.

Donkey rides on Blackheath have been as much a tradition as the fairs for the children of Greenwich. The same family has operated the donkey rides on the heath for over 120 years. Children can hop on a donkey just outside the main gates to the south of the park that open out onto the heath most summer weekends and Bank Holidays, just as in this picture from the early 1900s.

Boating Lake, Blackheath.

A much more serious sport could be found on Blackheath during the late 1700s when royalty, nobility and the general public gathered to participate in archery competitions. The sport had evolved when the gun replaced the longbow as a weapon of war. The longbow was in fact used as a weapon on Blackheath in 1497. Cornish archers gathered there after marching all the way from their home county ready to fight for the rights of the Cornish people rebelling against the English crown. The rebels were finally defeated when confronted by the king's men at Deptford Bridge. The old 'Dover Road', now Shooters Hill Road that runs across the heath, leads onto Shooters Hill once the main road into Kent. The name is thought to have associations with the archers who would practice their shooting nearby.

Opposite above: Boating on Blackheath at the turn of the twentieth century, one of the many ponds on the heath at that time. The pond just outside the park gates near the donkey rides would attract local residents as well as tourists who wanted to try out their boating skills. The ponds, although still there, no longer offer the attraction of a row on the water. Greenwich Park has a children's boating pond that is open during the summer months.

Opposite below: Youngsters would travel from all parts of London for a day's holiday in Greenwich. An illustration from 1897 depicts a group of East End boys on a day out fishing at one of the Blackheath ponds, many of which were hollows that were left after gravel was dug out and used as ballast for boats on the Thames.

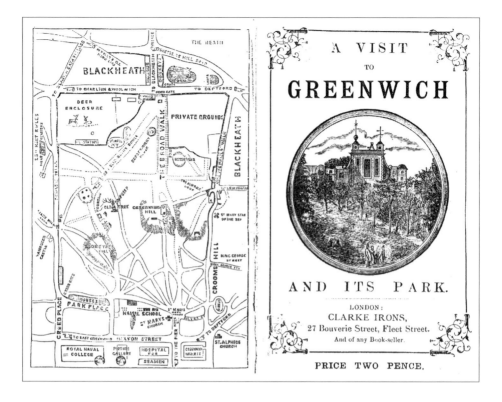

A VISIT
TO
GREENWICH

AND ITS PARK.

LONDON:
CLARKE IRONS,
27 Bouverie Street, Fleet Street.
And of any Book-seller.

PRICE TWO PENCE.

Thames may be had, with picturesque peeps at the Naval College and Observatory.

To the right is a nice grassy walk round the reservoir, a most secluded spot. At a short distance we once more enter the Broad Walk. If you now go as far as the Refreshment house you will be able to start on the best walk in the park, namely through

THE LONG GROVE ; when passing through this stately avenue there are times, especially on a misty day, that one can imagine one is quite fifty miles from London. This walk ends at a mound having a few seats at the foot of the trees growing there. This spot known as

QUEEN ELIZABETH'S BOWER, commands a pleasant view of the undulating ground around, and during the early mornings of spring, when the surrounding hawthorns are in blossom, this is one of the most delightful visiting places imaginable. The Princess Elizabeth (afterwards Queen), is said to have frequented this spot, and really made it her favorite resort ; from this fact it is named after her. From here it is a level walk to the famous

ONE TREE HILL, from whence other varied and delightful views may be had. Looking towards the Park walls, a mass of brick, ivy clad towers are to be seen, this heavy pile is

VANBRUGH CASTLE, a mansion built by Sir John Vanbrugh in the early part of last century, as a residence for himself. This gentleman was an architect, contemporary with Sir Christopher Wren, his building is all ponderous and grotesque, hence the epitaph written on him,

"Lie lightly on him earth,
  Though he laid many a heavy load on thee.

The building is now occupied as a young ladies' school. Descending One Tree Hill, which must be done with caution, we will go and have a look at

THE OLD TREE, standing in the hollow between this spot and the Observatory, whose dried and withered limbs stick grimly out from its sapless trunk, now clad with ivy. This old, time honoured tree is now fenced round and preserved as a memento of olden times, it having stood here for over eight centuries.*

We have now traversed nearly every portion of one of the prettiest and most compact Parks in England. But if one would know all its charms it must be visited in every season, its beauties being fully developed especially in Spring and Autumn.

Come hither then in the Spring of the year when the hawthorn trees are bedecked with their fragrant blossoms ; and when the pairing birds are singing their sweetest ; Come again in the heat of Summer when lads and lasses bound merrily over the green sward, while others sit in shaded and secluded spots whispering the oft repeated tales of love. Come again in the Autumn, when

* Two men, very old inhabitants of Greenwich, informed the writer that "they played around this tree when boys, the tree not being then fenced in ;" and the elder of these men said, "he could remember the trunk being hollowed out for Egerton, the park-keeper, and fitted with seats." A door was fixed at the entrance which completed the room, which served the park-keeper as a watch-house. It appears that boys broke certain rules of public order then as they do now, and the boys of those days who tormented the park-keeper were, when caught, locked in this hollow tree—my informant had been a culprit and had spent several hours of solitude in "Old Egerton's Cage."

The paddle steamer *Gibbon* loaded with Victorian day-trippers is just about to dock at Greenwich Pier. During the 1800s Greenwich was an extremely popular place to visit for people living up river, especially during Bank Holidays. With regular paddle steamer routes running back and forth from central London down to Greenwich and beyond, the tourists of the time could also take a river trip to see the sites of London or seaside towns such as Southend and Margate.

Opposite above: Greenwich, once part of Kent, has a royal park that gives visitors strolling through the leafy glades the feeling of being in the countryside once more. A pamphlet published during 1884 describes the parks attractions to visitors from the city, or indeed a resident living in the area during that time.

Opposite below: Inside, the pamphlet lists interesting places to see including the Deer Enclosure, Queen Elizabeth's Bower, the Observatory, and the Admiral's Poop! Information describes how one elderly Greenwich resident, when a young boy, was locked up in the tree for tormenting the park keeper. The Old tree, or Queen Elizabeth's Oak, was hollow and fitted with a small door.

A cover of a pamphlet from the early 1900s advertising Morton's Model Theatre where popular acts such as comedian Dan Leno and singer and dancer Kitty Fairdale performed. The theatre was demolished to make way for the new Greenwich Town Hall in 1937. Today the only theatre in Greenwich can be found on the site of the Rose and Crown Music Hall on Crooms Hill. Many public houses in Greenwich during the Victorian and Edwardian periods had small music-hall theatres on their premises to entertain their customers.

Opposite above: All classes visited Greenwich at the turn of the twentieth century with many taking in a show at one of Greenwich's popular theatres or music halls. The New Prince of Wales (later renamed the Carlton, the Theatre Royal, Mortons Model Theatre and the New Greenwich Theatre), was located on London Street (now the top end of Greenwich High Road). The theatre was built in 1864 to replace the derelict Theatre Royal in Deptford. The famous Victorian music-hall entertainer Arthur Lloyd performed at the theatre during the late 1880s.

Opposite below: Rowing was a favourite pastime for energetic young men of Greenwich. One of the oldest rowing clubs on the river, 'Curlew' has been based in Greenwich for over 130 years. Just along from the rowing club was Corbetts Boatyard where you could hire out all sorts of rowing boats for pleasure and competition. Races would take place all along the Thames from Limehouse to Blackwall Point, a place where pirates were hung in chains during the eighteenth century.

Greenwich beach in the late 1800s. On a sunny day a popular spot for local residents and day-trippers was a small stretch of sand and shingle just below the river walkway running from Greenwich Pier to the Trafalgar Tavern. Local workers and their families had little chance of relaxation so during the weekends when the tide was out Greenwich beach would be packed with people taking in the sunshine, picnicking or even going for a paddle in the water.

Opposite above: The most popular weekend pastime for the workers during the turn of the twentieth century was a visit to a football match. In 1886, a group of employees from the Royal Arsenal at Woolwich formed a team called Dial Square named after their place of work. By the early 1900s this works' team had gone on to become Woolwich Arsenal playing professional matches in the first division of the football league. This match at the Manor Ground, Plumstead was against Sheffield United in 1907.

Opposite below: Woolwich Arsenal football team attracted crowds in the thousands as seen here on the Spion Kop at the Manor Ground, Plumstead during the early 1900s. The majority of the spectators came from the local factories and industries in the area. They would work on Saturday mornings then finish by lunchtime ready for kick-off in the afternoon.

Arsenal V Sheffield United at Plumstead 2-3-07.

Section of the Crowd on Spion Kop, Manor Ground 22.9.06.

Match programme, *c.* 1908. Woolwich Arsenal had played at several grounds in the area, but strangely, although the club used Woolwich in their title, all the grounds they played home matches at were in Plumstead. Crowds of over 20,000 were attending matches during this time, but in 1913 when crowds started to dwindle, the club's owners decided to relocate to North London.

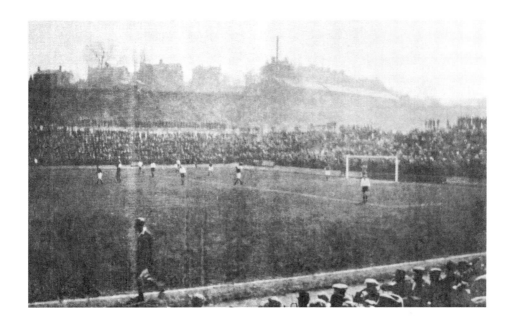

Above: In 1905 another football team from just along the river was formed by a group of local boys living in Lower Charlton. They called themselves Charlton Athletic and played their home matches at several grounds over the next fifteen years until just after the First World War. A move took the club to a more permanent home ground known as the Valley situated in disused chalk and sand pits. The local people helped level out a pitch and the workers in the area had another team to support. Home attendances, as seen in this picture from around the early 1920s were averaging around 7,500 – quite good for a team playing in the Third Division South.

Below: A view of the Valley from the 1920s. After just a few years playing matches there, the club's owners decided to relocate to Catford – it was a disaster. The club returned the next season playing once more at their spiritual home. The club moved again in the mid-1980s to ground share with Crystal Palace, then West Ham Utd, because of financial and ground safety problems at the Valley. After a vigorous campaign by supporters and the election of a new board of directors the club returned in 1992 to a refurbished stadium that will eventually have a capacity of up to 40,000.

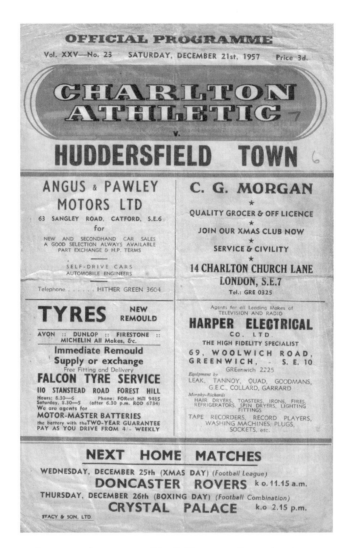

Programme cover from a match against Huddersfield Town in December 1957. During the 1957-58 season, Charlton Athletic played in one of the most dramatic matches in their history. Down to ten men and 5-1 down to their visitors, Charlton fought back in the second half, and were winning 6-5 until Huddersfield Town scored again. With a minute of the match remaining, Charlton Athletic hit the winner and the match finished with the score 7-6 to the home side.

seven

Family Roots

My own family ancestors have resided in Greenwich and the surrounding areas from at least the mid-1800s. At one time most would have lived and worked in close proximity to each other.

Today only a few family members still reside within the Borough of Greenwich. It seems that within modern society, opportunities are there to seek work and homes in all parts of the country, even the world.

Although I have also moved away from the place I was born, I still consider Greenwich my home.

Charles Ramzan, my grandfather, travelled from India by way of the Royal Navy in the early part of the 1900s. Serving for a while on HMS *Victory*, he eventually settled in Greenwich where he met and married Lillian Pearce whose family resided in the area. They had four children – David my father, Charlie, Marrian and Helen.

HMS *Victory*, my grandfather's ship, in the early part of the twentieth century. Moored off Portsmouth, Nelson's flagship was used as a training vessel for young sailors.

Lillian Pearce seated in the centre of the picture is accompanied by one of her bothers, Jim, and two sisters, Kit and Betty. My great-grandmother adopted Betty after she was born in the unmarried mothers' home in Poplar run by PC Robinson's sister.

Above: My grandfather on my mother's side of the family, Arthur Peachey, seen on the far right of the picture. A lorry driver by trade, he is standing with his co-workers from the local gasworks depot during the early 1900s. His mother, Susannah Angel, was the goddaughter of Charlie Peace. The Angel family had resided near Peckham, home of the master criminal whom they knew as the respectable Mr Ward, musician and inventor.

Left: Grandparents at a family wedding in the late 1960s. Hanna Kerrison's family originated from Ireland and when they journeyed to England they settled in Deptford, the neighbouring borough to Greenwich. Arthur Peachey met and married Hanna and remained in Deptford for all of their married lives. They had six children: Doreen my mother, Anne, Eileen, Arthur, Dennis and Ronnie.

Right: The family home in Old Woolwich Road, Greenwich. This was the original main road to Woolwich before the new road was built in 1825. The terraced houses were built in 1850 as part of the Morden College estates. Standing at the front door are my great-great-grandmother and great-grandmother with Betty, the adopted baby.

Below: The latest family members 2005, Elizabeth my daughter and sons Alex and Toby. Although all three were born in Kent and have no affinity to Greenwich, they enjoy our trips when I bring them home. They like playing in the park, hiring out a rowing boat on the pond, visiting the Maritime Museum or taking a walk along the Thames. Greenwich has changed considerably since I was as young as my children but it is still a very special place and is still the centre of the world.

Other local titles published by The History Press

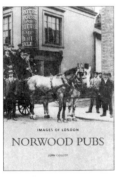

City of Westminster
BRIAN GIRLING

With over 200 old images, *City of Westminster* leads the reader around Pimlico through Belgravia and Knightsbridge, Mayfair and St James' and on to Soho and the West End's famous theatreland. There are pictures of vanished neighbourhoods, street characters, busy markets, trams, horse-drawn buses and old theatres. We see the Thames frozen, the Dorchester Hotel being built, suffragettes in Knightsbridge and an Edwardian driving school in Soho.

0 7524 3191 9

Norwood Pubs
JOHN COULTER

During the Victorian period there was an explosion in the number of newly built pubs and hotels in the London suburb of Norwood. Containing over 100 illustrations, this fascinating book captures the architecture of Norwood's Dickensian pubs and reveals each establishment's history. It will prove an informative and entertaining guide for anyone interested in the history of brewing in the area.

0 7524 3837 6

Eastenders' Postcards
GERALD GOSLING AND LES BERRY

This striking selection of old views from the capital city's East End combines popular sights with everyday scenes, from aerial views of Tower Bridge, the River Thames and London Docks, to vistas of terraced houses, shops and businesses. This valuable pictorial history will reawaken nostalgic memories for some, while offering a unique glimpse into the past for others.

0 7524 2494 7

London Inn Signs
JOAN P. ALCOCK

Illustrated with over 100 photographs, this history of signs from notable historic inns in London offers a fascinating insight into the history behind them. Joan Alcock takes the reader on a tour of many central London inns and also includes a brief general history of inn signs. An ideal gift for anyone wanting to follow a historic trail of London's inns and also particularly appealing to local history groups who organise such walks.

978 07524 3833 6

If you are interested in purchasing other books published by The History Press, or in case you have difficulty finding any of our books in your local bookshop, you can also place orders directly through our website

www.thehistorypress.co.uk